PAPER CRAFTS FOR ST. PATRICK'S DAY

Randel McGee

Enslow Element

an imprint of

Enslow Publishers, Inc.
40 Industrial Road
Box 398
Berkeley Heights, NJ 07922
USA

http://www.enslow.com

D1127701

Dedicated to the memory of John McGee. He left Ireland for the United States to join in the fight for independence during the Revolutionary War. He received a land grant in Pennsylvania and founded McGee's Mills. I am one of his descendants.

This book meets the National Standards for Arts Education.

Enslow Elementary, an imprint of Enslow Publishers, Inc.
Enslow Elementary® is a registered trademark of Enslow Publishers, Inc.

Library of Congress Cataloging-in-Publication Data

McGee, Randel.
  Paper crafts for St. Patrick's Day / Randel McGee.
      p. cm. — (Paper craft fun for holidays)
  Includes bibliographical references and index.
  Summary: "Explains the significance of St. Patrick's Day and how to make St. Patrick's Day themed crafts out of
      paper"—Provided by publisher.
  ISBN 978-0-7660-3725-0
  1. Saint Patrick's Day decorations—Juvenile literature. 2. Paper work—Juvenile literature. I. Title.
  TT900.S25M345 2012
  745.54—dc22
               2010024707

Paperback ISBN: 978-1-59845-337-9

Printed in the United States of America

052011 Lake Book Manufacturing, Inc., Melrose Park, IL

10 9 8 7 6 5 4 3 2 1

Illustration Credits: Crafts prepared by Randel McGee; photography by Enslow Publishers, Inc.; © Richard Levine/Alamy, p. 5.

Cover Illustration: Crafts prepared by Randel McGee; photography by Enslow Publishers, Inc.

CONTENTS

AUTHOR'S NOTE: Many of the materials used in making these crafts may be found by using recycled paper products. The author uses such recycled items as cereal boxes and similar packaging for light cardboard, manila folders for card stock paper, leftover pieces of wrapping paper, and so forth. This not only reduces the cost of the projects but is also a great way to reuse and recycle paper. Be sure to ask an adult for permission before using any recycled paper products.

The projects in this book were created for this particular holiday. However, I invite readers to be imaginative and find new ways to use the ideas in this book to create different projects of their own. Please feel free to share pictures of your work with me through www.mcgeeproductions.com. Happy Crafting!

ST. PATRICK'S DAY!

Maewyn Succat was a rowdy and reckless lad. His carefree life quickly changed when he was captured by fierce raiders and carried away to the wild land across the windy sea. He was sold as a slave and forced to tend sheep on lonely green hills. For six years he lived among strange people in a land far from home. One day he escaped, and, with luck and faith, he found his way to a ship sailing for his homeland. It took many weeks and lots of adventures, but he arrived home.

Maewyn decided to become a priest and took the Roman name Patricius. One night Patricius had a dream. He saw a man with a letter from the people of the wild land he had escaped. He heard the people of that land, Ireland, asking him to return to them and teach them the Christian faith. He did return to Ireland to teach the people. The Irish people called him Patrick.

Patrick traveled all around Ireland, building churches and schools and teaching the people the Christian faith. There were those who fought against Patrick and his beliefs, but he pushed forward with faith and courage. He became well loved for his service to the people.

Priests of that time often shaved the tops of their heads, so the Irish nicknamed Patrick "Old Shaved Head." He served in Ireland for more than thirty years and is generally believed to have died on March 17, in the late fifth century (sometime between 460–495 CE).

The Irish people honor St. Patrick's life on March 17. The first St. Patrick's Day parade was held in New York City in 1762. Many cities around the world now have special celebrations and parades on this day. This day celebrates not only St. Patrick but also Ireland and its people and culture. Wherever this day is celebrated, everyone, no matter where they are from, playfully becomes "Irish for the Day."

Ireland is called "the Emerald Isle" due to its green fields and forests. Green is the color traditionally worn on this day. The lucky three-leaved shamrock is a popular symbol of Ireland. Leprechauns, the "magical little people" of Irish folktales, also appear on this day . . . in decorations. On St. Patrick's Day, show your "Irish Spirit" with the decorations and costumes you can make from this book.

St. Patrick Figure

Patrick was not officially named a saint by a pope but was declared a saint by the people of Ireland for his love, devotion, and great works. It is told that he did amazing acts of a spiritual nature that strengthened the people's belief of his Christian teachings. We do not know for sure what he looked like, but he probably wore the robes and miter hat of a Catholic bishop when he was serving in the churches he founded.

What you will need

- ✎ tracing paper
- ✎ pencil
- ✎ white card stock
- ✎ crayons or markers
- ✎ construction paper in any color (optional)
- ✎ scissors
- ✎ clear tape

WHAT TO DO

1. Use tracing paper and a pencil to transfer the pattern from page 42 to white card stock.

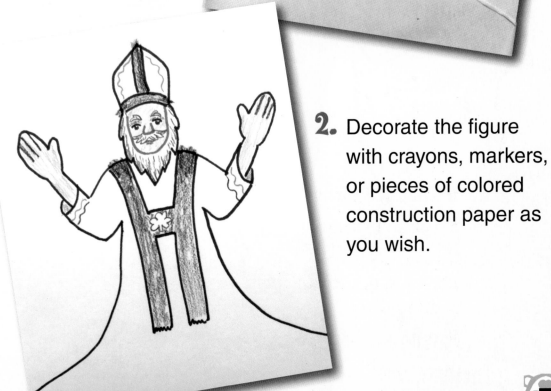

2. Decorate the figure with crayons, markers, or pieces of colored construction paper as you wish.

3. Cut out the pattern along the black outlines.

4. Fold the arms slightly forward.

5. Tape the sides of the robe together behind the figure.

6. Stand the figure up on a table or desk to watch over your St. Patrick's Day celebration.

Shamrock Chain

The shamrock is a three-leaved plant. The name comes from the Old Irish word *seamróg,* which means "little clover." The ancient Irish thought three was a lucky number. St. Patrick used the shamrock to explain religious concepts. The shamrock is considered a national emblem of Ireland and often appears on business signs, schools, sports teams' uniforms, and public offices. Bring the lucky, green shamrocks to your classroom, home, or party with this simple decorative chain.

What you will need

- tracing paper
- pencil
- construction paper
- scissors
- crayons or markers (optional)

WHAT TO DO

1. Use tracing paper and a pencil to transfer the pattern from page 43 to the construction paper.

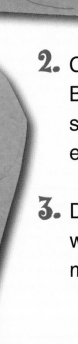

2. Cut out the pattern. Be sure to cut the small slit at the top of each pattern piece.

3. Decorate the pieces with crayons or markers if you wish.

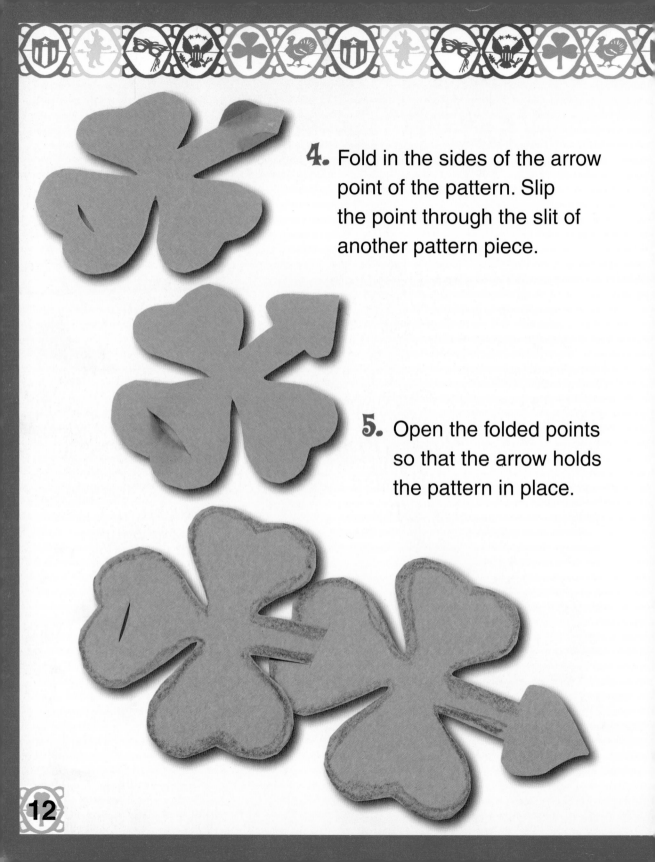

4. Fold in the sides of the arrow point of the pattern. Slip the point through the slit of another pattern piece.

5. Open the folded points so that the arrow holds the pattern in place.

6. Make enough pieces to form a chain.

Green Leprechaun Hat

There are tales about little fairy folk or leprechauns. The word comes from an Old Irish term *leath bhrógan,* which means "fairy shoemaker." According to legends, leprechauns are small gnome-like characters who make little shoes and collect golden treasures. They are quick-witted, quick-tempered, and quick on their feet! They have magical powers and can grant wishes, if a human is clever enough to capture one. They traditionally dress in green clothes with vests and top hats.

What you will need

- poster board— 14 x 8½ inches
- tracing paper
- pencil
- scissors
- crayons or markers
- construction paper—various colors

WHAT TO DO

1. Fold the poster board in half width-wise, like a book.

2. Use tracing paper and a pencil to transfer the pattern on page 41 to the poster board. Be sure to place the dotted line of the pattern on the fold.

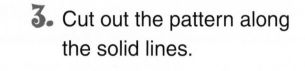

3. Cut out the pattern along the solid lines.

4. Decorate it with crayons or markers as you wish. Add a shamrock or ribbon from construction paper if you wish (see the shamrock pattern on page 43).

5. Gently push the bottom of the hat back and slip it on your head.

Pot o' Gold and Rainbow Pop-up Card

Irish legends claim that a leprechaun's pot of gold can be found where the end of the rainbow touches the ground. Share this colorful pop-up card with a friend!

What you will need

- white card stock
- tracing paper
- pencil
- scissors
- crayons or markers
- gold foil or wrapping paper (optional)
- white glue
- craft foam or cardboard (optional)
- cotton batting (optional)
- construction paper— any color

WHAT TO DO

1. Fold the white card stock in half width-wise, like a book.

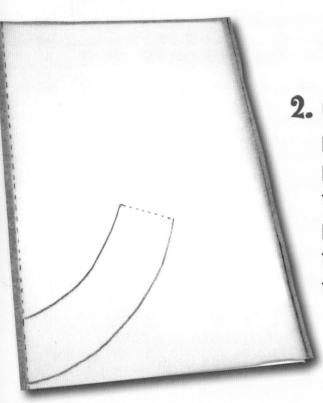

2. Use the tracing paper and pencil to copy the pattern from page 39 to card stock. Be sure to place the dotted line of the pattern on the fold. Transfer the pot pattern from page 41 to another piece of card stock.

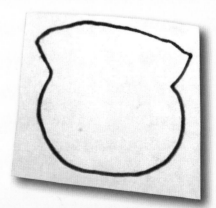

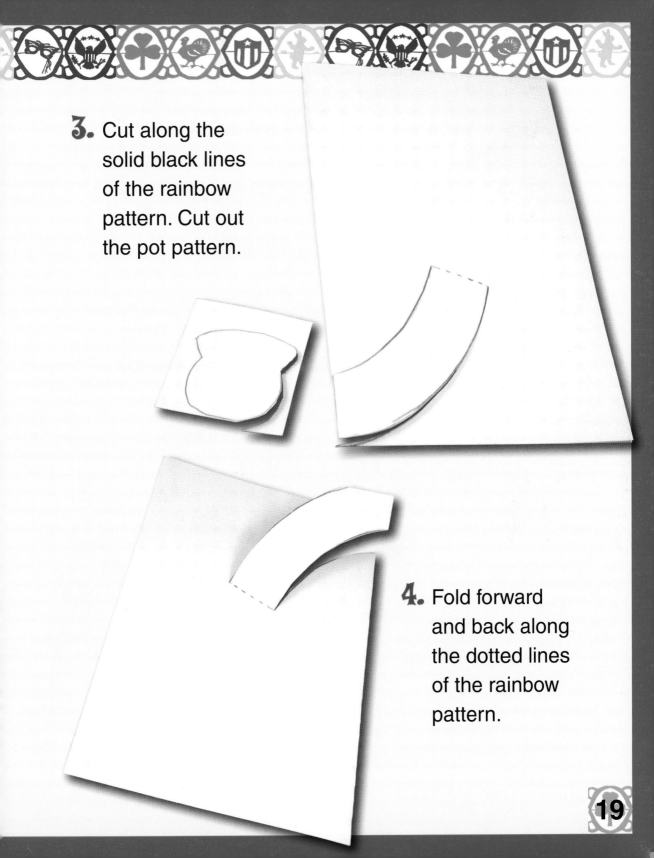

3. Cut along the solid black lines of the rainbow pattern. Cut out the pot pattern.

4. Fold forward and back along the dotted lines of the rainbow pattern.

5. Open the card and decorate it with crayons or markers as you wish. Color the pot and decorate it with some gold foil. Glue a small square of craft foam or cardboard on the back of the pot, and glue it at the end of the rainbow. Let dry.

6. Gently push the rainbow forward from the back, and fold the card closed. If you wish, glue little bits of cotton batting to the back of the rainbow to look like clouds.

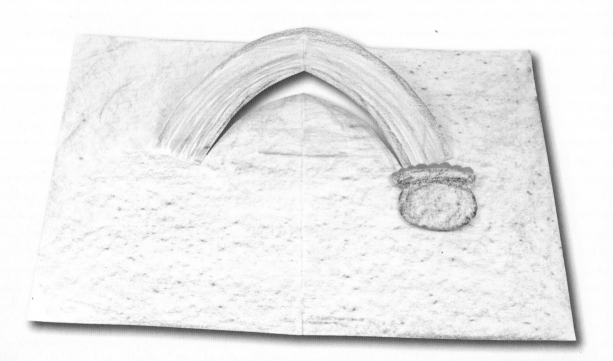

7. Glue the card stock to a piece of colored construction paper. Let dry.

8. Decorate the card and write a St. Patrick's Day greeting as you wish.

On this Saint Patrick's Day...

May the Luck o' the Irish be with You!

Cartoon Flip Book

Animated cartoons are a series of still pictures that are filmed in such a way that we see them as a moving picture. You can create the same effect by making a flip book. This is a series of simple sketches, changed slightly on each of the sixteen pages. When you flip through these pages with your thumb, the images seem to move. Let us look again at the idea of a pot of gold at the end of the rainbow for our cartoon.

What You Will Need

- ✎ white computer paper or white notepad paper
- ✎ scissors
- ✎ pencil and ruler
- ✎ colored pencils
- ✎ glue or stapler

What to Do

1. Cut the computer paper into sixteen 3-inch squares, or use notepad paper.

2. Number each piece of paper in the top left corner from 1 to 16.
3. Copy the patterns from page 43 to the first and last pages of your flip book squares.
4. Use a pencil to trace the figures from the first page on to each of the other pages, but change each picture just a bit. For example, move the eyes and arms with each picture and make the rainbow a bit longer in each picture. Have your last few pages look more like the last page of the pattern.

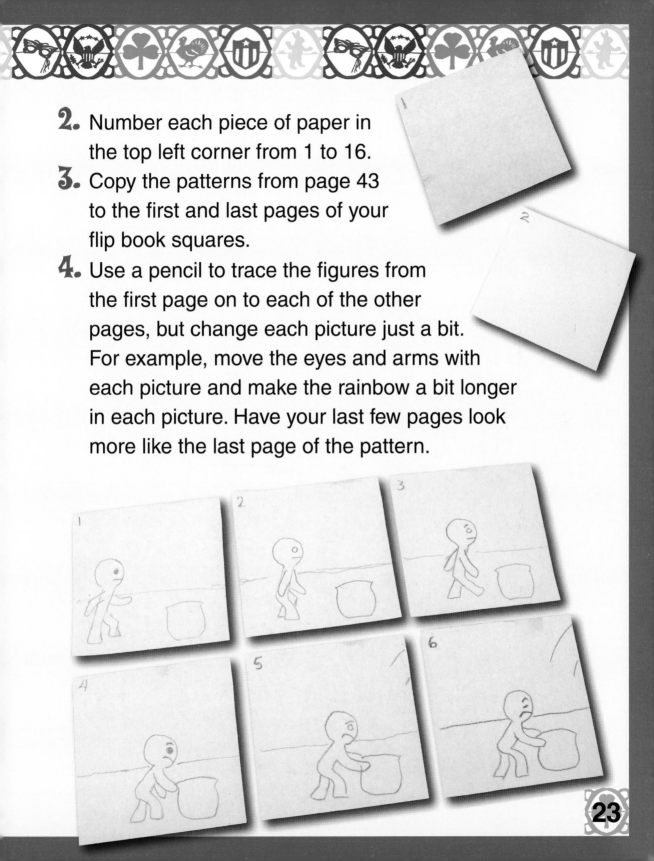

5. Use colored pencils to add a bit of color to each page. Add hair and clothes as you wish.

6. Glue or staple the pages along the left edge in order, with #1 on top and #16 on the bottom. Let the glue dry.

7. Hold the left edge of the flip book tightly in your hand, and flip through the pages with your right thumb. Watch the pictures move through a little leprechaun adventure!

LEPRECHAUN LIMBER JACK OR JILL

A limber jack is a jointed puppet on a stick that dances to lively Irish music. Traveling Irish street performers would sit on busy street corners and play a tin whistle in one hand and dance the puppet with the other. Make your limber jack, or jill, kick up its heels in a dance!

WHAT YOU WILL NEED

- tracing paper
- pencil
- cardboard
- scissors
- card stock
- toilet tissue tube
- green wrapping paper
- white glue

- hole punch
- crayons or markers
- construction paper in various colors
- tissue paper (optional)
- ruler
- string or yarn
- a 1/4-inch dowel, 12 inches long

WHAT TO DO

1. Use tracing paper and a pencil to transfer the arm and leg patterns from page 40 to the cardboard. Cut out the designs. Transfer the head design to the card stock.

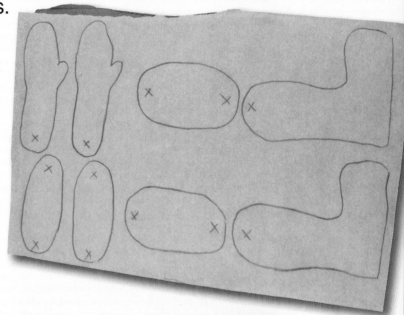

2. Wrap the toilet tissue tube with the green wrapping paper, and glue down all the loose edges.

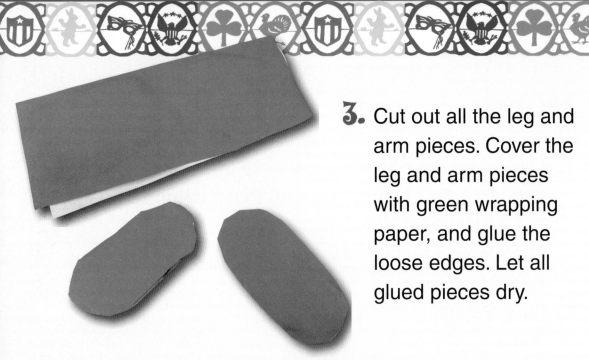

3. Cut out all the leg and arm pieces. Cover the leg and arm pieces with green wrapping paper, and glue the loose edges. Let all glued pieces dry.

4. Use the hole punch to make holes on both ends of the tube. Also make holes on the arm and leg pieces as shown.

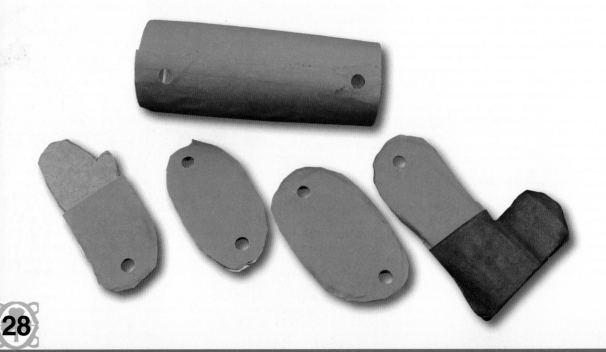

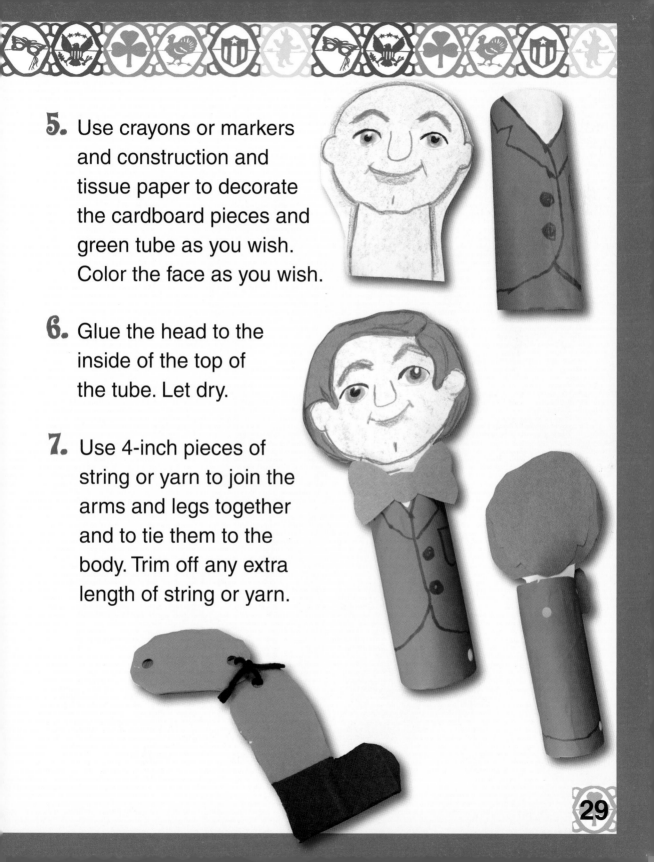

5. Use crayons or markers and construction and tissue paper to decorate the cardboard pieces and green tube as you wish. Color the face as you wish.

6. Glue the head to the inside of the top of the tube. Let dry.

7. Use 4-inch pieces of string or yarn to join the arms and legs together and to tie them to the body. Trim off any extra length of string or yarn.

8. Punch a hole in the back of the figure, and insert a 12-inch-long, ¼-inch-thick dowel into the hole. Glue it in place. Let it dry.

9. Hold the limber jack or jill so that its feet touch a table or desk. Move the puppet a little to make it dance.

CELTIC KNOT CHAIN NECKLACE

The Celts were the people who lived through much of ancient Europe, England, Scotland, and Ireland. The Celts made beautiful designs that looked like elaborate knots of rope or vines. They decorated their homes, furniture, utensils, clothes, and jewelry with these designs. This Celtic knot chain necklace is a simple version made with green paper. Green is one of the colors of the Irish flag and is considered a lucky color. People wear green to celebrate St. Patrick's Day.

WHAT YOU WILL NEED

- ✎ **green construction paper or green computer paper**
- ✎ **scissors**
- ✎ **tracing paper**
- ✎ **pencil and ruler**
- ✎ **crayons or markers**
- ✎ **clear tape**

What to Do

1. Cut green construction paper or computer paper into rectangles 8½ x 5½ inches.

2. Fold the green paper in half lengthwise.

3. Use tracing paper and a pencil to transfer the pattern from page 41 to green paper. You should be able to get four chain links from each rectangle. Be sure to put the smaller end of the pattern on the fold.

4. Cut out at least sixteen links for the chain. Decorate them with crayons or markers as you wish.

5. Open a folded chain link, and slightly fold the large end of that link to slip it through the large opening of another link.

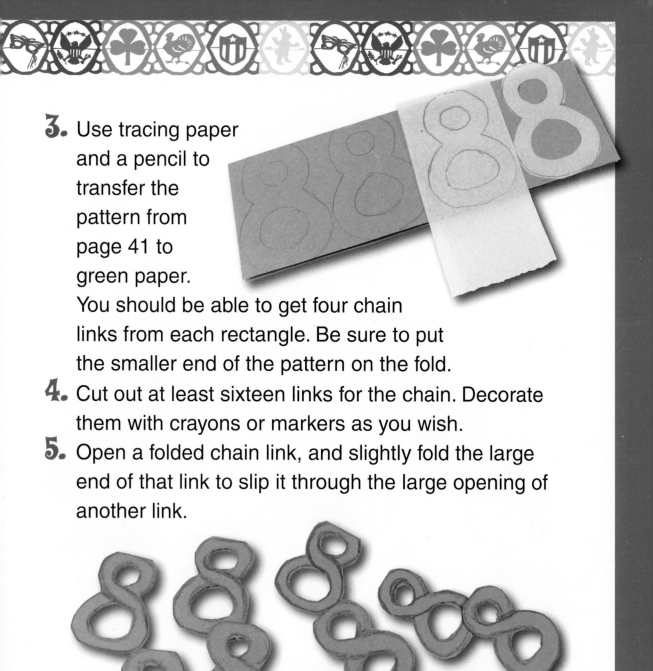

6. Continue linking the pieces together until you have a long chain.

7. Tape the two ends of the chain together.

8. Carefully place the chain around your neck.

IRISH SYMBOLS MOBILE

Some special symbols that many people associate with Ireland are the Irish flag of green, white, and orange, representing Catholics, Protestants, and their unity; the Celtic harp, a popular symbol of the music of Ireland; and the shamrock, the three-leaved emblem of St. Patrick and Ireland. This mobile uses these symbols and maps of the Republic of Ireland and Northern Ireland to honor the Irish and their culture.

WHAT YOU WILL NEED

- ✎ **computer paper**
- ✎ **white glue**
- ✎ **light cardboard**
- ✎ **crayons or markers**
- ✎ **scissors and ruler**
- ✎ **hole punch**
- ✎ **string or yarn**
- ✎ **a 1/4-inch dowel, 12 inches long**

What to do

1. Transfer the designs from page 44 to computer paper.

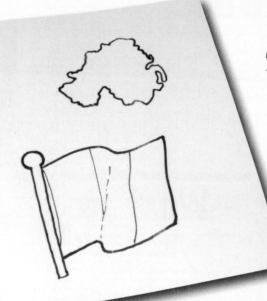

2. Glue the computer paper design to light cardboard. Let dry.

3. Use crayons or markers to color the designs as you wish.

4. Cut out the designs. Punch a hole on the places marked with an X.

5. Use different lengths of string or yarn (3 inches to 7 inches) to tie the designs to the dowel.

6. Tie an 18-inch string to the middle of the dowel as the hanging line. Be sure to balance the weight of the designs on the dowel so that it hangs rather evenly.

7. Have an adult help you hang the mobile.

PATTERNS

The percentages included on the patterns tell you how much to enlarge or shrink the image using a copier. Most copiers and printers have an adjustable size/percentage feature to change the size of an image when you print it. After you print the patterns to their true sizes, cut them out or use tracing paper to copy them. Ask an adult to help you trace and cut the shapes.

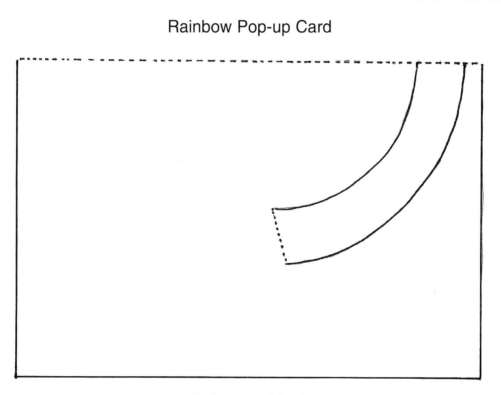

Rainbow Pop-up Card

Enlarge 165%

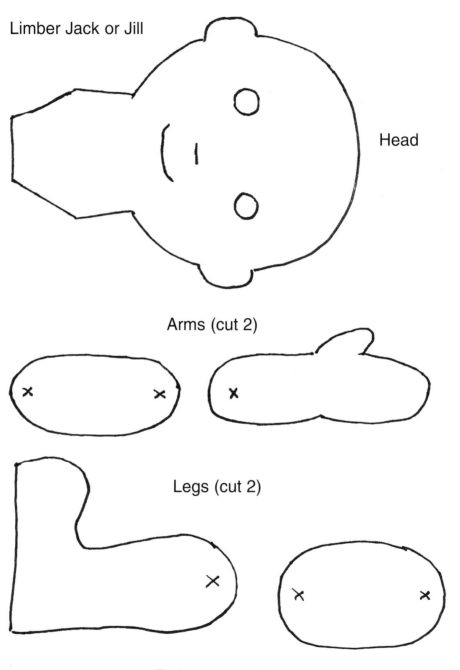

Limber Jack or Jill

Head

Arms (cut 2)

Legs (cut 2)

Enlarge 145%

Rainbow and Pot o' Gold Pop-up Card

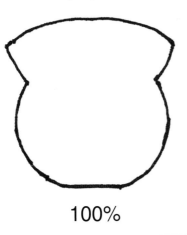

100%

Celtic Chain

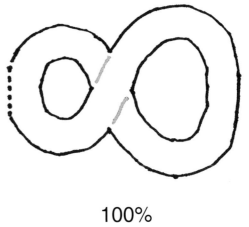

100%

Leprechaun Hat

Enlarge 200%

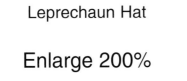

St. Patrick Figure

Enlarge
155%

Cartoon Flip Book First Page

Cartoon Flip Book Last Page

Enlarge 120%

Shamrock Symbol

Enlarge 250%

Shamrock Chain

Enlarge 180%

Outline of the Republic of Ireland

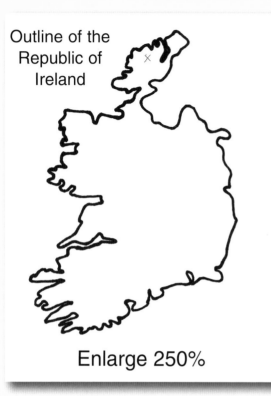

Enlarge 250%

Celtic Harp Symbol

Enlarge 145%

Outline of Northern Ireland

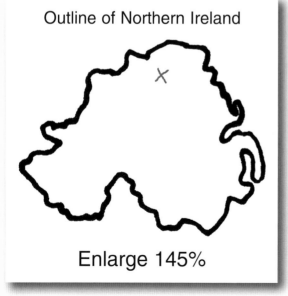

Enlarge 145%

Flag of Ireland

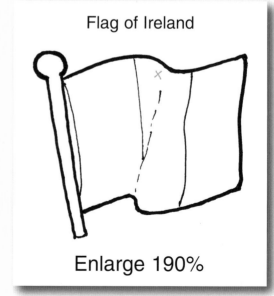

Enlarge 190%

READ ABOUT

Books

Aloian, Molly. *St. Patrick's Day.* New York: Crabtree Publishing Company, 2010.

Wade, Mary Dodson. *Ireland: A Question and Answer Book.* Mankato, Minn.: Capstone Press, 2007.

Internet Addresses

DLTK's: Saint Patrick's Day Activities
<http://www.dltk-holidays.com/patrick/index.html>

Kaboose: St. Patrick's Day 2012
<http://holidays.kaboose.com/saint-patricks-day/>

FamilyFun: St. Patrick's Day Crafts Ideas
<http://familyfun.go.com/st-patricks-day/st-patricks-day-crafts>

Visit Randel McGee's Web site at
<http://www.mcgeeproductions.com>

INDEX

ABOUT THE AUTHOR

Randel McGee has been playing with paper and scissors for as long as he can remember. As soon as he was able to get a library card, he would go to the library and find the books that showed paper crafts, check them out, take them home, and try almost every craft in the book. He still checks out books on paper crafts at the library, but he also buys books to add to his own library and researches paper-craft sites on the Internet.

McGee says, "I begin by making copies of simple crafts or designs I see in books. Once I get the idea of how something is made, I begin to make changes to make the designs more personal. After a lot of trial and error, I find ways to do something new and different that is all my own. That's when the fun begins!"

McGee has also liked singing and acting from a young age. He graduated from college with a degree in children's theater and specialized in puppetry. After college, he taught himself ventriloquism and started performing at libraries and schools with a friendly dragon puppet named Groark. "Randel McGee and Groark" have toured throughout the

United States and Asia, sharing their fun shows with young and old alike. Groark is the star of two award-winning video series for elementary school students on character education: *Getting Along With Groark* and *The Six Pillars of Character*.

In the 1990s, McGee combined his love of making things with paper with his love of telling stories. He tells stories while making pictures cut from paper to illustrate the tales he tells. The famous author Hans Christian Andersen also made cut-paper pictures when he told stories. McGee portrays Andersen in storytelling performances around the world.

Besides performing and making things, McGee, with the help of his wife, Marsha, likes showing librarians, teachers, fellow artists, and children the fun and educational experiences they can have with paper crafts, storytelling, drama, and puppetry. Randel McGee has belonged to the Guild of American Papercutters, the National Storytelling Network, and the International Ventriloquists' Association. He has been a regional director for the Puppeteers of America, Inc., and past president of UNIMA-USA, an international puppetry organization. He has been active in working with children and scouts in his community and church for many years. He and his wife live in California. They are the parents of five grown children who are all talented artists and performers.